Answers from God's Word

❧

compiled by
John Dingman and Kit Sublett

Whitecaps Media
HOUSTON

Whitecaps Media
P. O. Box 60385
Houston, TX 77205-0385
Website: www.whitecapsmedia.com
E-mail: whitecapsmedia@earthlink.net

Dedicated to the Campaigner kids of Young Life in the Northwest
Houston Area, past, present, and future

ISBN-13: 978-0-9758577-4-8
ISBN-10: 0-9758577-4-6

For information on bulk sales of this book, contact Whitecaps Media
at the above address

Printed in the United States of America

Every word of God proves true ...
(Proverbs 30:5)

The Bible is God's written revelation to mankind and provides us with incomparable wisdom and insight.

In this little book you will find verses on dozens of topics, ranging from everyday matters to matters of eternity. These selections are not exhaustive, but will give you a place to start studying these topics.

We hope that the book will encourage you to delve deeper into the Bible, and develop the habit of turning to God's Word for answers, inspiration, and guidance.

A NOTE ABOUT PUNCTUATION: Many verses are parts of sentences that begin or end in another verse (for example, 1 Thessalonians 5:17). In such cases we have shown the complete verse, beginning or ending with an ellipsis (...) to reflect the missing part of the sentence.

If only part of a verse is shown, the reference will reflect it (John 14:31a, for example).

Contents

Anger

James 1:19–20
Know this, my beloved brothers: let every person be quick
to hear, slow to speak, slow to anger; for the anger of man
does not produce the righteousness that God requires.

Ephesians 4:31–32
Let all bitterness and wrath and anger and clamor and
slander be put away from you, along with all malice. Be
kind to one another, tenderhearted, forgiving one another,
as God in Christ forgave you.

Colossians 3:8
But now you must put them all away: anger, wrath, malice,
slander, and obscene talk from your mouth.

Psalm 37:8
Refrain from anger, and forsake wrath!
    Fret not yourself; it tends only to evil.

Ephesians 4:26–27
Be angry and do not sin; do not let the sun go down on
your anger, and give no opportunity to the devil.

Proverbs 22:24–25
Make no friendship with a man given to anger,
    nor go with a wrathful man,
lest you learn his ways
    and entangle yourself in a snare.

Matthew 5:21–22
"You have heard that it was said to those of old, 'You
shall not murder; and whoever murders will be liable to
judgment.' But I say to you that everyone who is angry with

his brother will be liable to judgment; whoever insults his brother will be liable to the council; and whoever says, 'You fool!' will be liable to the hell of fire."

ASSURANCE OF SALVATION

John 10:28–29
"I give them eternal life, and they will never perish, and no one will snatch them out of my hand. My Father, who has given them to me, is greater than all, and no one is able to snatch them out of the Father's hand."

1 John 5:11–12
And this is the testimony, that God gave us eternal life, and this life is in his Son. Whoever has the Son has life; whoever does not have the Son of God does not have life.

John 6:40
"For this is the will of my Father, that everyone who looks on the Son and believes in him should have eternal life, and I will raise him up on the last day."

Ephesians 2:8–9
For by grace you have been saved through faith. And this is not your own doing; it is the gift of God, not a result of works, so that no one may boast.

Romans 11:29
For the gifts and the calling of God are irrevocable.

1 Peter 1:3–5
Blessed be the God and Father of our Lord Jesus Christ! According to his great mercy, he has caused us to be

born again to a living hope through the resurrection of Jesus Christ from the dead, to an inheritance that is imperishable, undefiled, and unfading, kept in heaven for you, who by God's power are being guarded through faith for a salvation ready to be revealed in the last time.

Romans 8:38–39
For I am sure that neither death nor life, nor angels nor rulers, nor things present nor things to come, nor powers, nor height nor depth, nor anything else in all creation, will be able to separate us from the love of God in Christ Jesus our Lord.

John 3:36
"Whoever believes in the Son has eternal life; whoever does not obey the Son shall not see life, but the wrath of God remains on him."

Authority

Romans 13:1
Let every person be subject to the governing authorities. For there is no authority except from God, and those that exist have been instituted by God.

1 Peter 2:13–17
Be subject for the Lord's sake to every human institution, whether it be to the emperor as supreme, or to governors as sent by him to punish those who do evil and to praise those who do good. For this is the will of God, that by doing good you should put to silence the ignorance of foolish people. Live as people who are free, not using your freedom as a cover-up for evil, but living as servants of God. Honor

everyone. Love the brotherhood. Fear God. Honor the emperor.

Titus 3:1
Remind them to be submissive to rulers and authorities, to be obedient, to be ready for every good work ...

Ephesians 6:1
Children, obey your parents in the Lord, for this is right.

Colossians 3:22
Slaves, obey in everything those who are your earthly masters, not by way of eye-service, as people-pleasers, but with sincerity of heart, fearing the Lord.

Becoming A Christian

Romans 10:9–10
... because, if you confess with your mouth that Jesus is Lord and believe in your heart that God raised him from the dead, you will be saved. For with the heart one believes and is justified, and with the mouth one confesses and is saved.

John 6:40
"For this is the will of my Father, that everyone who looks on the Son and believes in him should have eternal life, and I will raise him up on the last day."

Ephesians 2:8–9
For by grace you have been saved through faith. And this is not your own doing; it is the gift of God, not a result of works, so that no one may boast.

Acts 16:31
And they said, "Believe in the Lord Jesus, and you will be saved, you and your household."

Acts 4:12
"And there is salvation in no one else, for there is no other name under heaven given among men by which we must be saved."

John 1:12–13
But to all who did receive him, who believed in his name, he gave the right to become children of God, who were born, not of blood nor of the will of the flesh nor of the will of man, but of God.

Titus 3:5
… he saved us, not because of works done by us in righteousness, but according to his own mercy, by the washing of regeneration and renewal of the Holy Spirit …

Acts 2:21
"'And it shall come to pass that everyone who calls upon the name of the Lord shall be saved.'"

Romans 3:23–24
… for all have sinned and fall short of the glory of God, and are justified by his grace as a gift, through the redemption that is in Christ Jesus …

2 Corinthians 5:21
For our sake he made him to be sin who knew no sin, so that in him we might become the righteousness of God.

Acts 13:38–39
Let it be known to you therefore, brothers, that through this man forgiveness of sins is proclaimed to you, and by him

everyone who believes is freed from everything from which you could not be freed by the law of Moses.

John 14:6
Jesus said to him, "I am the way, and the truth, and the life. No one comes to the Father except through me."

John 6:44
"No one can come to me unless the Father who sent me draws him. And I will raise him up on the last day."

1 John 5:11–12
And this is the testimony, that God gave us eternal life, and this life is in his Son. Whoever has the Son has life; whoever does not have the Son of God does not have life.

John 3:3
Jesus answered him, "Truly, truly, I say to you, unless one is born again he cannot see the kingdom of God."

The Bible (see *God's Word*)

Church

Ephesians 1:22–23
And he put all things under his feet and gave him as head over all things to the church, which is his body, the fullness of him who fills all in all.

Ephesians 2:19–20
So then you are no longer strangers and aliens, but you

are fellow citizens with the saints and members of the household of God, built on the foundation of the apostles and prophets, Christ Jesus himself being the cornerstone...

1 Timothy 3:15
... if I delay, you may know how one ought to behave in the household of God, which is the church of the living God, a pillar and buttress of truth.

Romans 12:4–5
For as in one body we have many members, and the members do not all have the same function, so we, though many, are one body in Christ, and individually members one of another.

Ephesians 4:16
... from whom the whole body, joined and held together by every joint with which it is equipped, when each part is working properly, makes the body grow so that it builds itself up in love.

James 2:1–4
My brothers, show no partiality as you hold the faith in our Lord Jesus Christ, the Lord of glory. For if a man wearing a gold ring and fine clothing comes into your assembly, and a poor man in shabby clothing also comes in, and if you pay attention to the one who wears the fine clothing and say, "You sit here in a good place," while you say to the poor man, "You stand over there," or, "Sit down at my feet," have you not then made distinctions among yourselves and become judges with evil thoughts?

Matthew 18:20
"For where two or three are gathered in my name, there am I among them."

Acts 2:42–47
And they devoted themselves to the apostles' teaching
and fellowship, to the breaking of bread and the prayers.
And awe came upon every soul, and many wonders and
signs were being done through the apostles. And all who
believed were together and had all things in common. And
they were selling their possessions and belongings and
distributing the proceeds to all, as any had need. And day
by day, attending the temple together and breaking bread
in their homes, they received their food with glad and
generous hearts, praising God and having favor with all
the people. And the Lord added to their number day by day
those who were being saved.

Acts 9:31
So the church throughout all Judea and Galilee and
Samaria had peace and was being built up. And walking in
the fear of the Lord and in the comfort of the Holy Spirit, it
multiplied.

CONFLICT BETWEEN FRIENDS

1 Peter 4:8
Above all, keep loving one another earnestly, since love
covers a multitude of sins.

2 Timothy 2:24
And the Lord's servant must not be quarrelsome but kind
to everyone, able to teach, patiently enduring evil …

Philippians 2:14
Do all things without grumbling or questioning …

Ephesians 4:31–32
Let all bitterness and wrath and anger and clamor and slander be put away from you, along with all malice. Be kind to one another, tenderhearted, forgiving one another, as God in Christ forgave you.

Ephesians 4:1–3
I therefore, a prisoner for the Lord, urge you to walk in a manner worthy of the calling to which you have been called, with all humility and gentleness, with patience, bearing with one another in love, eager to maintain the unity of the Spirit in the bond of peace.

Colossians 3:13
… bearing with one another and, if one has a complaint against another, forgiving each other; as the Lord has forgiven you, so you also must forgive.

1 Thessalonians 5:11
Therefore encourage one another and build one another up, just as you are doing.

1 John 4:11–12
Beloved, if God so loved us, we also ought to love one another. No one has ever seen God; if we love one another, God abides in us and his love is perfected in us.

Galatians 6:1
Brothers, if anyone is caught in any transgression, you who are spiritual should restore him in a spirit of gentleness. Keep watch on yourself, lest you too be tempted.

Matthew 18:15–17
"If your brother sins against you, go and tell him his fault, between you and him alone. If he listens to you, you have gained your brother. But if he does not listen, take one

or two others along with you, that every charge may be established by the evidence of two or three witnesses. If he refuses to listen to them, tell it to the church. And if he refuses to listen even to the church, let him be to you as a Gentile and a tax collector."

Matthew 5:22
"But I say to you that everyone who is angry with his brother will be liable to judgment; whoever insults his brother will be liable to the council; and whoever says, 'You fool!' will be liable to the hell of fire."

Matthew 18:21–22
Then Peter came up and said to him, "Lord, how often will my brother sin against me, and I forgive him? As many as seven times?" Jesus said to him, "I do not say to you seven times, but seventy times seven."

Matthew 5:23–24
"So if you are offering your gift at the altar and there remember that your brother has something against you, leave your gift there before the altar and go. First be reconciled to your brother, and then come and offer your gift."

Hebrews 12:14–15
Strive for peace with everyone, and for the holiness without which no one will see the Lord. See to it that no one fails to obtain the grace of God; that no "root of bitterness" springs up and causes trouble, and by it many become defiled . . .

Dating

2 Corinthians 6:14
Do not be unequally yoked with unbelievers. For what partnership has righteousness with lawlessness? Or what fellowship has light with darkness?

1 Corinthians 15:33
Do not be deceived: "Bad company ruins good morals."

2 Timothy 2:22
So flee youthful passions and pursue righteousness, faith, love, and peace, along with those who call on the Lord from a pure heart.

1 Thessalonians 4:3–5
For this is the will of God, your sanctification: that you abstain from sexual immorality; that each one of you know how to control his own body in holiness and honor, not in the passion of lust like the Gentiles who do not know God...

Song of Songs 2:7
I adjure you, O daughters of Jerusalem,
    by the gazelles or the does of the field,
that you not stir up or awaken love
    until it pleases.

1 Corinthians 13:4–7
Love is patient and kind; love does not envy or boast; it is not arrogant or rude. It does not insist on its own way; it is not irritable or resentful; it does not rejoice at wrongdoing, but rejoices with the truth. Love bears all things, believes all things, hopes all things, endures all things.

DEATH

1 Corinthians 15:22
For as in Adam all die, so also in Christ shall all be made alive.

John 3:16
"For God so loved the world, that he gave his only Son, that whoever believes in him should not perish but have eternal life."

John 11:25–26
Jesus said to her, "I am the resurrection and the life. Whoever believes in me, though he die, yet shall he live, and everyone who lives and believes in me shall never die. Do you believe this?"

Romans 6:5
For if we have been united with him in a death like his, we shall certainly be united with him in a resurrection like his.

2 Corinthians 5:1
For we know that if the tent, which is our earthly home, is destroyed, we have a building from God, a house not made with hands, eternal in the heavens.

Hebrews 2:14–15
Since therefore the children share in flesh and blood, he himself likewise partook of the same things, that through death he might destroy the one who has the power of death, that is, the devil, and deliver all those who through fear of death were subject to lifelong slavery.

Romans 5:12
Therefore, just as sin came into the world through one

man, and death through sin, and so death spread to all men because all sinned ...

Ecclesiastes 8:8a
No man has power to retain the spirit, or power over the day of death.

Isaiah 25:8
He will swallow up death forever;
    and the Lord God will wipe away tears from all faces,
and the reproach of his people he will take away from all
        the earth,
for the Lord has spoken.

Revelation 21:4
"He will wipe away every tear from their eyes, and death shall be no more, neither shall there be mourning nor crying nor pain anymore, for the former things have passed away."

Hebrews 9:27
And just as it is appointed for man to die once, and after that comes judgment ...

Disappointment

Psalm 55:22
Cast your burden on the Lord,
    and he will sustain you;
he will never permit
    the righteous to be moved.

Romans 8:28
And we know that for those who love God all things work together for good, for those who are called according to his purpose.

1 Thessalonians 5:18
… give thanks in all circumstances; for this is the will of God in Christ Jesus for you.

2 Corinthians 4:8–10
We are afflicted in every way, but not crushed; perplexed, but not driven to despair; persecuted, but not forsaken; struck down, but not destroyed; always carrying in the body the death of Jesus, so that the life of Jesus may also be manifested in our bodies.

John 16:20
"Truly, truly, I say to you, you will weep and lament, but the world will rejoice. You will be sorrowful, but your sorrow will turn into joy."

Psalm 57:1
Be merciful to me, O God, be merciful to me,
    for in you my soul takes refuge;
in the shadow of your wings I will take refuge,
    till the storms of destruction pass by.

Romans 8:38–39
For I am sure that neither death nor life, nor angels nor rulers, nor things present nor things to come, nor powers, nor height nor depth, nor anything else in all creation, will be able to separate us from the love of God in Christ Jesus our Lord.

Divorce (see *Marriage and Divorce*)

Drinking

Ephesians 5:18
And do not get drunk with wine, for that is debauchery, but be filled with the Spirit ...

1 Peter 4:3
The time that is past suffices for doing what the Gentiles want to do, living in sensuality, passions, drunkenness, orgies, drinking parties, and lawless idolatry.

Romans 13:13
Let us walk properly as in the daytime, not in orgies and drunkenness, not in sexual immorality and sensuality, not in quarreling and jealousy.

Galatians 5:19–21
Now the works of the flesh are evident: sexual immorality, impurity, sensuality, idolatry, sorcery, enmity, strife, jealousy, fits of anger, rivalries, dissensions, divisions, envy, drunkenness, orgies, and things like these. I warn you, as I warned you before, that those who do such things will not inherit the kingdom of God.

Hebrews 4:15
For we do not have a high priest who is unable to sympathize with our weaknesses, but one who in every respect has been tempted as we are, yet without sin.

Romans 13:1–2
Let every person be subject to the governing authorities. For there is no authority except from God, and those that exist have been instituted by God. Therefore whoever resists the authorities resists what God has appointed, and those who resist will incur judgment.

Faith

Hebrews 11:1
Now faith is the assurance of things hoped for, the conviction of things not seen.

Mark 9:23
And Jesus said to him, "If you can! All things are possible for one who believes."

Matthew 21:22
"And whatever you ask in prayer, you will receive, if you have faith."

Hebrews 11:6
And without faith it is impossible to please him, for whoever would draw near to God must believe that he exists and that he rewards those who seek him.

Mark 2:5
And when Jesus saw their faith, he said to the paralytic, "My son, your sins are forgiven."

Mark 5:34
And he said to her, "Daughter, your faith has made you well; go in peace, and be healed of your disease."

Luke 17:6
And the Lord said, "If you had faith like a grain of mustard seed, you could say to this mulberry tree, 'Be uprooted and planted in the sea,' and it would obey you."

Romans 10:17
So faith comes from hearing, and hearing through the word of Christ.

James 2:17
So also faith by itself, if it does not have works, is dead.

Galatians 3:26
… for in Christ Jesus you are all sons of God, through faith.

Fellowship

Hebrews 10:24–25
And let us consider how to stir up one another to love and good works, not neglecting to meet together, as is the habit of some, but encouraging one another, and all the more as you see the Day drawing near.

Proverbs 27:17
Iron sharpens iron,
    and one man sharpens another.

Romans 12:10
Love one another with brotherly affection. Outdo one another in showing honor.

Hebrews 3:13
But exhort one another every day, as long as it is called "today," that none of you may be hardened by the deceitfulness of sin.

Galatians 6:2
Bear one another's burdens, and so fulfill the law of Christ.

Romans 14:1
As for the one who is weak in faith, welcome him, but not to quarrel over opinions.

1 Peter 3:8
Finally, all of you, have unity of mind, sympathy, brotherly love, a tender heart, and a humble mind.

Acts 2:42–47
And they devoted themselves to the apostles' teaching and fellowship, to the breaking of bread and the prayers. And awe came upon every soul, and many wonders and signs were being done through the apostles. And all who believed were together and had all things in common. And they were selling their possessions and belongings and distributing the proceeds to all, as any had need. And day by day, attending the temple together and breaking bread in their homes, they received their food with glad and generous hearts, praising God and having favor with all the people. And the Lord added to their number day by day those who were being saved.

Forgiveness

Ephesians 1:7–8
In him we have redemption through his blood, the forgiveness of our trespasses, according to the riches of his grace, which he lavished upon us, in all wisdom and insight …

Psalm 103:12
… as far as the east is from the west,
    so far does he remove our transgressions from us.

1 John 1:9–10
If we confess our sins, he is faithful and just to forgive us our sins and to cleanse us from all unrighteousness. If we

say we have not sinned, we make him a liar, and his word is not in us.

Colossians 3:13
… bearing with one another and, if one has a complaint against another, forgiving each other; as the Lord has forgiven you, so you also must forgive.

Isaiah 43:25
"I, I am he
  who blots out your transgressions for my own sake,
  and I will not remember your sins."

Psalm 32:5
I acknowledged my sin to you,
  and I did not cover my iniquity;
I said, "I will confess my transgressions to the LORD,"
  and you forgave the iniquity of my sin.

FRUSTRATION AND PATIENCE

Proverbs 16:32
Whoever is slow to anger is better than the mighty,
  and he who rules his spirit than he who takes a city.

Galatians 5:22–23
But the fruit of the Spirit is love, joy, peace, patience, kindness, goodness, faithfulness, gentleness, self-control; against such things there is no law.

Proverbs 14:29
Whoever is slow to anger has great understanding,
  but he who has a hasty temper exalts folly.

Romans 12:12
Rejoice in hope, be patient in tribulation, be constant in prayer.

Ephesians 4:2
... with all humility and gentleness, with patience, bearing with one another in love ...

Romans 5:3–5
More than that, we rejoice in our sufferings, knowing that suffering produces endurance, and endurance produces character, and character produces hope, and hope does not put us to shame, because God's love has been poured into our hearts through the Holy Spirit who has been given to us.

Galatians 6:9
And let us not grow weary of doing good, for in due season we will reap, if we do not give up.

Colossians 3:12–13
Put on then, as God's chosen ones, holy and beloved, compassion, kindness, humility, meekness, and patience, bearing with one another and, if one has a complaint against another, forgiving each other; as the Lord has forgiven you, so you also must forgive.

Isaiah 40:30–31
Even youths shall faint and be weary,
    and young men shall fall exhausted;
but they who wait for the Lord shall renew their strength;
    they shall mount up with wings like eagles;
they shall run and not be weary;
    they shall walk and not faint.

1 Corinthians 13:4
Love is patient and kind; love does not envy or boast; it is not arrogant ...

GIVING

Luke 6:38
"... give, and it will be given to you. Good measure, pressed down, shaken together, running over, will be put into your lap. For with the measure you use it will be measured back to you."

Matthew 5:42
"Give to the one who begs from you, and do not refuse the one who would borrow from you."

2 Corinthians 9:7, 11
Each one must give as he has made up his mind, not reluctantly or under compulsion, for God loves a cheerful giver.
    You will be enriched in every way for all your generosity, which through us will produce thanksgiving to God.

Proverbs 11:24–25
One gives freely, yet grows all the richer;
    another withholds what he should give, and only suffers
        want.
Whoever brings blessing will be enriched,
    and one who waters will himself be watered.

Matthew 6:1–4
"Beware of practicing your righteousness before other people in order to be seen by them, for then you will have

no reward from your Father who is in heaven.

"Thus, when you give to the needy, sound no trumpet before you, as the hypocrites do in the synagogues and in the streets, that they may be praised by others. Truly, I say to you, they have received their reward. But when you give to the needy, do not let your left hand know what your right hand is doing, so that your giving may be in secret. And your Father who sees in secret will reward you."

Proverbs 3:9–10
Honor the LORD with your wealth
   and with the firstfruits of all your produce;
then your barns will be filled with plenty,
   and your vats will be bursting with wine.

Proverbs 22:9
Whoever has a bountiful eye will be blessed,
   for he shares his bread with the poor.

GOD'S CHARACTER

Psalm 147:5
Great is our Lord, and abundant in power;
   his understanding is beyond measure.

Psalm 100:5
For the LORD is good;
   his steadfast love endures forever,
   and his faithfulness to all generations.

1 John 1:5
This is the message we have heard from him and proclaim to you, that God is light, and in him is no darkness at all.

Psalm 18:30
This God—his way is perfect;
   the word of the LORD proves true;
   he is a shield for all those who take refuge in him.

Psalm 89:8
O LORD God of hosts,
   who is mighty as you are, O LORD,
   with your faithfulness all around you?

Acts 17:24
The God who made the world and everything in it, being
Lord of heaven and earth, does not live in temples made by
man ...

Numbers 23:19
God is not man, that he should lie,
   or a son of man, that he should change his mind.
Has he said, and will he not do it?
   Or has he spoken, and will he not fulfill it?

1 John 4:7
Beloved, let us love one another, for love is from God, and
whoever loves has been born of God and knows God.

James 1:17
Every good gift and every perfect gift is from above, coming
down from the Father of lights with whom there is no
variation or shadow due to change.

1 John 4:8
Anyone who does not love does not know God, because
God is love.

1 Samuel 15:29
"And also the Glory of Israel will not lie or have regret, for

he is not a man, that he should have regret."

Psalm 33:4
For the word of the Lord is upright,
   and all his work is done in faithfulness.

Psalm 9:7
But the Lord sits enthroned forever;
   he has established his throne for justice …

God's Will

Romans 12:2
Do not be conformed to this world, but be transformed by the renewal of your mind, that by testing you may discern what is the will of God, what is good and acceptable and perfect.

Psalm 18:30
This God—his way is perfect;
   the word of the Lord proves true;
   he is a shield for all those who take refuge in him.

1 Thessalonians 5:18
… give thanks in all circumstances; for this is the will of God in Christ Jesus for you.

Romans 8:28
And we know that for those who love God all things work together for good, for those who are called according to his purpose.

Matthew 26:42
Again, for the second time, he went away and prayed, "My Father, if this cannot pass unless I drink it, your will be done."

John 10:10
"The thief comes only to steal and kill and destroy. I came that they may have life and have it abundantly."

Jeremiah 29:11
For I know the plans I have for you, declares the LORD, plans for wholeness and not for evil, to give you a future and a hope.

1 John 2:17
And the world is passing away along with its desires, but whoever does the will of God abides forever.

Psalm 135:6
Whatever the LORD pleases, he does,
    in heaven and on earth,
    in the seas and all deeps.

Proverbs 16:9
The heart of man plans his way,
    but the LORD establishes his steps.

1 Peter 2:15
For this is the will of God, that by doing good you should put to silence the ignorance of foolish people.

Isaiah 46:10
"... declaring the end from the beginning
    and from ancient times things not yet done,
saying, 'My counsel shall stand,
    and I will accomplish all my purpose' ..."

God's Word

Isaiah 40:8
The grass withers, the flower fades,
    but the word of our God will stand forever.

Proverbs 30:5
Every word of God proves true;
    he is a shield to those who take refuge in him.

Joshua 1:8
This Book of the Law shall not depart from your mouth,
but you shall meditate on it day and night, so that you may
be careful to do according to all that is written in it. For
then you will make your way prosperous, and then you will
have good success.

2 Timothy 3:16–17
All Scripture is breathed out by God and profitable for
teaching, for reproof, for correction, and for training in
righteousness, that the man of God may be competent,
equipped for every good work.

Hebrews 4:12
For the word of God is living and active, sharper than any
two-edged sword, piercing to the division of soul and of
spirit, of joints and of marrow, and discerning the thoughts
and intentions of the heart.

James 1:22–25
But be doers of the word, and not hearers only, deceiving
yourselves. For if anyone is a hearer of the word and not a
doer, he is like a man who looks intently at his natural face
in a mirror. For he looks at himself and goes away and at
once forgets what he was like. But the one who looks into

the perfect law, the law of liberty, and perseveres, being no hearer who forgets but a doer who acts, he will be blessed in his doing.

Psalm 119:9–11
How can a young man keep his way pure?
    By guarding it according to your word.
With my whole heart I seek you;
    let me not wander from your commandments!
I have stored up your word in my heart,
    that I might not sin against you.

John 20:30–31
Now Jesus did many other signs in the presence of the disciples, which are not written in this book; but these are written so that you may believe that Jesus is the Christ, the Son of God, and that by believing you may have life in his name.

2 Peter 1:21
For no prophecy was ever produced by the will of man, but men spoke from God as they were carried along by the Holy Spirit.

Good Works

Matthew 5:16
In the same way, let your light shine before others, so that they may see your good works and give glory to your Father who is in heaven.

Ephesians 2:8–10
For by grace you have been saved through faith. And

this is not your own doing; it is the gift of God, not a result of works, so that no one may boast. For we are his workmanship, created in Christ Jesus for good works, which God prepared beforehand, that we should walk in them.

James 2:17–18
So also faith by itself, if it does not have works, is dead.

But someone will say, "You have faith and I have works." Show me your faith apart from your works, and I will show you my faith by my works.

1 Timothy 6:18
They are to do good, to be rich in good works, to be generous and ready to share ...

Hebrews 13:16
Do not neglect to do good and to share what you have, for such sacrifices are pleasing to God.

Ephesians 4:11–13
And he gave the apostles, the prophets, the evangelists, the pastors and teachers, to equip the saints for the work of ministry, for building up the body of Christ, until we all attain to the unity of the faith and of the knowledge of the Son of God, to mature manhood, to the measure of the stature of the fullness of Christ ...

1 Peter 2:12
Keep your conduct among the Gentiles honorable, so that when they speak against you as evildoers, they may see your good deeds and glorify God on the day of visitation.

1 Timothy 5:25
So also good works are conspicuous, and even those that are not cannot remain hidden.

James 4:17
So whoever knows the right thing to do and fails to do it,
for him it is sin.

Growing In Christ

2 Corinthians 5:17
Therefore, if anyone is in Christ, he is a new creation. The
old has passed away; behold, the new has come.

Colossians 2:6–7
Therefore, as you received Christ Jesus the Lord, so walk
in him, rooted and built up in him and established in the
faith, just as you were taught, abounding in thanksgiving.

Galatians 2:20
I have been crucified with Christ. It is no longer I who live,
but Christ who lives in me. And the life I now live in the
flesh I live by faith in the Son of God, who loved me and
gave himself for me.

1 Timothy 4:12
Let no one despise you for your youth, but set the believers
an example in speech, in conduct, in love, in faith, in
purity.

Ephesians 4:17–20
Now this I say and testify in the Lord, that you must no
longer walk as the Gentiles do, in the futility of their
minds. They are darkened in their understanding, alienated
from the life of God because of the ignorance that is in
them, due to their hardness of heart. They have become
callous and have given themselves up to sensuality, greedy

to practice every kind of impurity. But that is not the way you learned Christ!

Ephesians 2:19
So then you are no longer strangers and aliens, but you are fellow citizens with the saints and members of the household of God ...

2 Timothy 3:16–17
All Scripture is breathed out by God and profitable for teaching, for reproof, for correction, and for training in righteousness, that the man of God may be competent, equipped for every good work.

John 14:21
"Whoever has my commandments and keeps them, he it is who loves me. And he who loves me will be loved by my Father, and I will love him and manifest myself to him."

Heaven

John 14:1–3
"Let not your hearts be troubled. Believe in God; believe also in me. In my Father's house are many rooms. If it were not so, would I have told you that I go to prepare a place for you? And if I go and prepare a place for you, I will come again and will take you to myself, that where I am you may be also."

Philippians 3:20–21
But our citizenship is in heaven, and from it we await a Savior, the Lord Jesus Christ, who will transform our lowly body to be like his glorious body, by the power that enables

him even to subject all things to himself.

1 Corinthians 2:9
But, as it is written,
"What no eye has seen, nor ear heard,
    nor the heart of man imagined,
    what God has prepared for those who love him."

Hebrews 12:22–23
But you have come to Mount Zion and to the city of the living God, the heavenly Jerusalem, and to innumerable angels in festal gathering, and to the assembly of the firstborn who are enrolled in heaven, and to God, the judge of all, and to the spirits of the righteous made perfect ...

Revelation 21:3–4
And I heard a loud voice from the throne saying, "Behold, the dwelling place of God is with man. He will dwell with them, and they will be his people, and God himself will be with them as their God. He will wipe away every tear from their eyes, and death shall be no more, neither shall there be mourning nor crying nor pain anymore, for the former things have passed away."

Revelation 22:3–5
No longer will there be anything accursed, but the throne of God and of the Lamb will be in it, and his servants will worship him. They will see his face, and his name will be on their foreheads. And night will be no more. They will need no light of lamp or sun, for the Lord God will be their light, and they will reign forever and ever.

Luke 23:43
And he said to him, "Truly, I say to you, today you will be with me in Paradise."

Matthew 13:44
"The kingdom of heaven is like treasure hidden in a field, which a man found and covered up. Then in his joy he goes and sells all that he has and buys that field.

The Holy Spirit

John 14:26
"But the Helper, the Holy Spirit, whom the Father will send in my name, he will teach you all things and bring to your remembrance all that I have said to you."

John 14:16–17
"And I will ask the Father, and he will give you another Helper, to be with you forever, even the Spirit of truth, whom the world cannot receive, because it neither sees him nor knows him. You know him, for he dwells with you and will be in you."

John 16:7–11
"Nevertheless, I tell you the truth: it is to your advantage that I go away, for if I do not go away, the Helper will not come to you. But if I go, I will send him to you. And when he comes, he will convict the world concerning sin and righteousness and judgment: concerning sin, because they do not believe in me; concerning righteousness, because I go to the Father, and you will see me no longer; concerning judgment, because the ruler of this world is judged."

Ezekiel 36:27
And I will put my Spirit within you, and cause you to walk in my statutes and be careful to obey my rules.

1 Corinthians 3:16
Do you not know that you are God's temple and that God's Spirit dwells in you?

Romans 8:9
You, however, are not in the flesh but in the Spirit, if in fact the Spirit of God dwells in you. Anyone who does not have the Spirit of Christ does not belong to him.

Romans 5:5
… and hope does not put us to shame, because God's love has been poured into our hearts through the Holy Spirit who has been given to us.

2 Corinthians 5:5
He who has prepared us for this very thing is God, who has given us the Spirit as a guarantee.

1 Corinthians 2:10–14
… these things God has revealed to us through the Spirit. For the Spirit searches everything, even the depths of God. For who knows a person's thoughts except the spirit of that person, which is in him? So also no one comprehends the thoughts of God except the Spirit of God. Now we have received not the spirit of the world, but the Spirit who is from God, that we might understand the things freely given us by God. And we impart this in words not taught by human wisdom but taught by the Spirit, interpreting spiritual truths to those who are spiritual.

    The natural person does not accept the things of the Spirit of God, for they are folly to him, and he is not able to understand them because they are spiritually discerned.

Jesus

Hebrews 1:3
He is the radiance of the glory of God and the exact imprint of his nature, and he upholds the universe by the word of his power. After making purification for sins, he sat down at the right hand of the Majesty on high ...

Colossians 1:15–17
He is the image of the invisible God, the firstborn of all creation. For by him all things were created, in heaven and on earth, visible and invisible, whether thrones or dominions or rulers or authorities—all things were created through him and for him. And he is before all things, and in him all things hold together.

Colossians 2:9–10
For in him the whole fullness of deity dwells bodily, and you have been filled in him, who is the head of all rule and authority.

Matthew 3:16–17
And when Jesus was baptized, immediately he went up from the water, and behold, the heavens were opened to him, and he saw the Spirit of God descending like a dove and coming to rest on him; and behold, a voice from heaven said, "This is my beloved Son, with whom I am well pleased."

John 10:30
"I and the Father are one."

John 10:10
"The thief comes only to steal and kill and destroy. I came that they may have life and have it abundantly."

John 14:6
Jesus said to him, "I am the way, and the truth, and the life. No one comes to the Father except through me."

Hebrews 13:8
Jesus Christ is the same yesterday and today and forever.

Hebrews 4:15
For we do not have a high priest who is unable to sympathize with our weaknesses, but one who in every respect has been tempted as we are, yet without sin.

1 Corinthians 15:3–5
For I delivered to you as of first importance what I also received: that Christ died for our sins in accordance with the Scriptures, that he was buried, that he was raised on the third day in accordance with the Scriptures, and that he appeared to Cephas, then to the twelve.

1 Peter 3:18
For Christ also suffered once for sins, the righteous for the unrighteous, that he might bring us to God, being put to death in the flesh but made alive in the spirit ...

Philippians 2:6–11
... who, though he was in the form of God, did not count equality with God a thing to be grasped, but made himself nothing, taking the form of a servant, being born in the likeness of men. And being found in human form, he humbled himself by becoming obedient to the point of death, even death on a cross. Therefore God has highly exalted him and bestowed on him the name that is above every name, so that at the name of Jesus every knee should bow, in heaven and on earth and under the earth, and every tongue confess that Jesus Christ is Lord, to the glory of God the Father.

1 Timothy 2:5
For there is one God, and there is one mediator between God and men, the man Christ Jesus …

Acts 4:12
"And there is salvation in no one else, for there is no other name under heaven given among men by which we must be saved."

Living the Christian Life

John 3:30
"He must increase, but I must decrease."

Romans 12:1–2
I appeal to you therefore, brothers, by the mercies of God, to present your bodies as a living sacrifice, holy and acceptable to God, which is your spiritual worship. Do not be conformed to this world, but be transformed by the renewal of your mind, that by testing you may discern what is the will of God, what is good and acceptable and perfect.

Matthew 16:24–26
Then Jesus told his disciples, "If anyone would come after me, let him deny himself and take up his cross and follow me. For whoever would save his life will lose it, but whoever loses his life for my sake will find it. For what will it profit a man if he gains the whole world and forfeits his life? Or what shall a man give in return for his life?"

1 Peter 4:3–4
The time that is past suffices for doing what the Gentiles want to do, living in sensuality, passions, drunkenness,

orgies, drinking parties, and lawless idolatry. With respect
to this they are surprised when you do not join them in the
same flood of debauchery, and they malign you ...

1 Peter 1:15–16
... but as he who called you is holy, you also be holy in all
your conduct, since it is written, "You shall be holy, for I am
holy."

Galatians 2:20
I have been crucified with Christ. It is no longer I who live,
but Christ who lives in me. And the life I now live in the
flesh I live by faith in the Son of God, who loved me and
gave himself for me.

Romans 8:28
And we know that for those who love God all things work
together for good, for those who are called according to his
purpose.

Proverbs 3:5–6
Trust in the Lord with all your heart,
    and do not lean on your own understanding.
In all your ways acknowledge him,
    and he will make straight your paths.

LOVE

Matthew 22:37–39
And he said to him, "You shall love the Lord your God with
all your heart and with all your soul and with all your mind.
This is the great and first commandment. And a second is
like it: You shall love your neighbor as yourself."

Luke 6:27–28
"But I say to you who hear, Love your enemies, do good to those who hate you, bless those who curse you, pray for those who abuse you."

1 John 3:16
By this we know love, that he laid down his life for us, and we ought to lay down our lives for the brothers.

1 John 3:18
Little children, let us not love in word or talk but in deed and in truth.

John 14:31a
"... but I do as the Father has commanded me, so that the world may know that I love the Father."

Song of Songs 8:7
Many waters cannot quench love,
    neither can floods drown it.
If a man offered for love
    all the wealth of his house,
    he would be utterly despised.

Proverbs 10:12
Hatred stirs up strife,
    but love covers all offenses.

John 13:34–35
"A new commandment I give to you, that you love one another: just as I have loved you, you also are to love one another. By this all people will know that you are my disciples, if you have love for one another."

1 Corinthians 13:1–3
If I speak in the tongues of men and of angels, but have not love, I am a noisy gong or a clanging cymbal. And if I have prophetic powers, and understand all mysteries and all knowledge, and if I have all faith, so as to remove mountains, but have not love, I am nothing. If I give away all I have, and if I deliver up my body to be burned, but have not love, I gain nothing.

1 Corinthians 13:4–8
Love is patient and kind; love does not envy or boast; it is not arrogant or rude. It does not insist on its own way; it is not irritable or resentful; it does not rejoice at wrongdoing, but rejoices with the truth. Love bears all things, believes all things, hopes all things, endures all things.

Love never ends. As for prophecies, they will pass away; as for tongues, they will cease; as for knowledge, it will pass away.

Marriage and Divorce

Genesis 2:24
Therefore a man shall leave his father and his mother and hold fast to his wife, and they shall become one flesh.

Mark 10:6–9
"But from the beginning of creation, 'God made them male and female.' 'Therefore a man shall leave his father and mother and hold fast to his wife, and they shall become one flesh.' So they are no longer two but one flesh. What therefore God has joined together, let not man separate."

Proverbs 18:22
He who finds a wife finds a good thing
   and obtains favor from the LORD.

2 Corinthians 6:14–15
Do not be unequally yoked with unbelievers. For what
partnership has righteousness with lawlessness? Or what
fellowship has light with darkness? What accord has Christ
with Belial? Or what portion does a believer share with an
unbeliever?

Hebrews 13:4
Let marriage be held in honor among all, and let the
marriage bed be undefiled, for God will judge the sexually
immoral and adulterous.

1 Peter 3:7
Likewise, husbands, live with your wives in an
understanding way, showing honor to the woman as the
weaker vessel, since they are heirs with you of the grace of
life, so that your prayers may not be hindered.

Ephesians 5:21–23
… submitting to one another out of reverence for Christ.
Wives, submit to your own husbands, as to the Lord. For
the husband is the head of the wife even as Christ is the
head of the church, his body, and is himself its Savior.

Matthew 19:3–9
And Pharisees came up to him and tested him by asking,
"Is it lawful to divorce one's wife for any cause?" He
answered, "Have you not read that he who created them
from the beginning made them male and female, and said,
'Therefore a man shall leave his father and his mother
and hold fast to his wife, and they shall become one flesh'?
So they are no longer two but one flesh. What therefore

God has joined together, let not man separate." They said to him, "Why then did Moses command one to give a certificate of divorce and to send her away?" He said to them, "Because of your hardness of heart Moses allowed you to divorce your wives, but from the beginning it was not so. And I say to you: whoever divorces his wife, except for sexual immorality, and marries another, commits adultery."

1 Corinthians 7:10–17
To the married I give this charge (not I, but the Lord): the wife should not separate from her husband (but if she does, she should remain unmarried or else be reconciled to her husband), and the husband should not divorce his wife.

To the rest I say (I, not the Lord) that if any brother has a wife who is an unbeliever, and she consents to live with him, he should not divorce her. If any woman has a husband who is an unbeliever, and he consents to live with her, she should not divorce him. For the unbelieving husband is made holy because of his wife, and the unbelieving wife is made holy because of her husband. Otherwise your children would be unclean, but as it is, they are holy. But if the unbelieving partner separates, let it be so. In such cases the brother or sister is not enslaved. God has called you to peace. Wife, how do you know whether you will save your husband? Husband, how do you know whether you will save your wife?

Only let each person lead the life that the Lord has assigned to him, and to which God has called him. This is my rule in all the churches.

1 Corinthians 7:27
Are you bound to a wife? Do not seek to be free. Are you free from a wife? Do not seek a wife.

Money And Possessions

Psalm 24:1
The earth is the Lord's and the fullness thereof,
  the world and those who dwell therein ...

Luke 16:13
"No servant can serve two masters, for either he will hate
the one and love the other, or he will be devoted to the one
and despise the other. You cannot serve God and money."

1 Timothy 6:10
For the love of money is a root of all kinds of evils. It is
through this craving that some have wandered away from
the faith and pierced themselves with many pangs.

Hebrews 13:5
Keep your life free from love of money, and be content with
what you have, for he has said, "I will never leave you nor
forsake you."

Proverbs 22:1
A good name is to be chosen rather than great riches,
  and favor is better than silver or gold.

Luke 12:15
And he said to them, "Take care, and be on your guard
against all covetousness, for one's life does not consist in
the abundance of his possessions."

Luke 12:48b
"Everyone to whom much was given, of him much will be
required, and from him to whom they entrusted much,
they will demand the more."

NEW CHRISTIANS

John 1:12–13
But to all who did receive him, who believed in his name, he gave the right to become children of God, who were born, not of blood nor of the will of the flesh nor of the will of man, but of God.

2 Corinthians 5:17
Therefore, if anyone is in Christ, he is a new creation. The old has passed away; behold, the new has come.

1 John 5:11–12
And this is the testimony, that God gave us eternal life, and this life is in his Son. Whoever has the Son has life; whoever does not have the Son of God does not have life.

Ephesians 2:8–9
For by grace you have been saved through faith. And this is not your own doing; it is the gift of God, not a result of works, so that no one may boast.

1 Peter 4:3–4
The time that is past suffices for doing what the Gentiles want to do, living in sensuality, passions, drunkenness, orgies, drinking parties, and lawless idolatry. With respect to this they are surprised when you do not join them in the same flood of debauchery, and they malign you ...

Ephesians 2:19–20
So then you are no longer strangers and aliens, but you are fellow citizens with the saints and members of the household of God, built on the foundation of the apostles and prophets, Christ Jesus himself being the cornerstone...

Galatians 2:20
I have been crucified with Christ. It is no longer I who live, but Christ who lives in me. And the life I now live in the flesh I live by faith in the Son of God, who loved me and gave himself for me.

Ephesians 4:20–23
But that is not the way you learned Christ!—assuming that you have heard about him and were taught in him, as the truth is in Jesus, to put off your old self, which belongs to your former manner of life and is corrupt through deceitful desires, and to be renewed in the spirit of your minds …

Colossians 3:12
Put on then, as God's chosen ones, holy and beloved, compassion, kindness, humility, meekness, and patience…

1 Timothy 4:12
Let no one despise you for your youth, but set the believers an example in speech, in conduct, in love, in faith, in purity.

2 Timothy 2:22–24
So flee youthful passions and pursue righteousness, faith, love, and peace, along with those who call on the Lord from a pure heart. Have nothing to do with foolish, ignorant controversies; you know that they breed quarrels. And the Lord's servant must not be quarrelsome but kind to everyone, able to teach, patiently enduring evil …

Other Religions

John 14:6
Jesus said to him, "I am the way, and the truth, and the life. No one comes to the Father except through me."

Acts 4:12
"And there is salvation in no one else, for there is no other name under heaven given among men by which we must be saved."

1 John 2:22–23
Who is the liar but he who denies that Jesus is the Christ? This is the antichrist, he who denies the Father and the Son. No one who denies the Son has the Father. Whoever confesses the Son has the Father also.

Galatians 1:8
But even if we or an angel from heaven should preach to you a gospel contrary to the one we preached to you, let him be accursed.

Romans 1:18–19
For the wrath of God is revealed from heaven against all ungodliness and unrighteousness of men, who by their unrighteousness suppress the truth. For what can be known about God is plain to them, because God has shown it to them.

Psalm 10:13
Why does the wicked renounce God
   and say in his heart, "You will not call to account"?

Colossians 2:8
See to it that no one takes you captive by philosophy and

empty deceit, according to human tradition, according to the elemental spirits of the world, and not according to Christ.

Deuteronomy 18:10
There shall not be found among you anyone who burns his son or his daughter as an offering, anyone who practices divination or tells fortunes or interprets omens, or a sorcerer ...

Deuteronomy 4:2
You shall not add to the word that I command you, nor take from it, that you may keep the commandments of the LORD your God that I command you.

Deuteronomy 12:32
"Everything that I command you, you shall be careful to do. You shall not add to it or take from it."

Proverbs 30:5–6
Every word of God proves true;
   he is a shield to those who take refuge in him.
Do not add to his words,
   lest he rebuke you and you be found a liar.

Parents

Exodus 20:12
"Honor your father and your mother, that your days may be long in the land that the LORD your God is giving you."

Ephesians 6:1–4
Children, obey your parents in the Lord, for this is

right. "Honor your father and mother" (this is the first commandment with a promise), "that it may go well with you and that you may live long in the land." Fathers, do not provoke your children to anger, but bring them up in the discipline and instruction of the Lord.

Proverbs 10:1
A wise son makes a glad father,
    but a foolish son is a sorrow to his mother.

Colossians 3:20
Children, obey your parents in everything, for this pleases the Lord.

Proverbs 23:22
Listen to your father who gave you life,
    and do not despise your mother when she is old.

Psalm 27:10
For my father and my mother have forsaken me,
    but the Lord will take me in.

Psalm 68:5
Father of the fatherless and protector of widows
    is God in his holy habitation.

Proverbs 3:12
… for the Lord reproves him whom he loves,
    as a father the son in whom he delights.

Proverbs 17:6
Grandchildren are the crown of the aged,
    and the glory of children is their fathers.

Patience (see *Frustration and Patience*)

Pornography

Psalm 101:3–4
I will not set before my eyes
   anything that is worthless.
I hate the work of those who fall away;
   it shall not cling to me.
A perverse heart shall be far from me;
   I will know nothing of evil.

Psalm 119:37
Turn my eyes from looking at worthless things;
   and give me life in your ways.

Matthew 5:27–30
"You have heard that it was said, 'You shall not commit adultery.' But I say to you that everyone who looks at a woman with lustful intent has already committed adultery with her in his heart. If your right eye causes you to sin, tear it out and throw it away. For it is better that you lose one of your members than that your whole body be thrown into hell. And if your right hand causes you to sin, cut it off and throw it away. For it is better that you lose one of your members than that your whole body go into hell."

James 1:13–15
Let no one say when he is tempted, "I am being tempted by God," for God cannot be tempted with evil, and he himself tempts no one. But each person is tempted when he is lured and enticed by his own desire. Then desire when it has conceived gives birth to sin, and sin when it is fully grown brings forth death.

1 Corinthians 10:13
No temptation has overtaken you that is not common to

man. God is faithful, and he will not let you be tempted beyond your ability, but with the temptation he will also provide the way of escape, that you may be able to endure it.

Ephesians 4:17–19
Now this I say and testify in the Lord, that you must no longer walk as the Gentiles do, in the futility of their minds. They are darkened in their understanding, alienated from the life of God because of the ignorance that is in them, due to their hardness of heart. They have become callous and have given themselves up to sensuality, greedy to practice every kind of impurity.

1 John 2:15–16
Do not love the world or the things in the world. If anyone loves the world, the love of the Father is not in him. For all that is in the world—the desires of the flesh and the desires of the eyes and pride in possessions—is not from the Father but is from the world.

Prayer

John 15:7
"If you abide in me, and my words abide in you, ask whatever you wish, and it will be done for you."

Luke 18:1
And he told them a parable to the effect that they ought always to pray and not lose heart.

Matthew 18:19–20
"Again I say to you, if two of you agree on earth about

anything they ask, it will be done for them by my Father in heaven. For where two or three are gathered in my name, there am I among them."

James 1:6–7
But let him ask in faith, with no doubting, for the one who doubts is like a wave of the sea that is driven and tossed by the wind. For that person must not suppose that he will receive anything from the Lord …

John 14:13–14
"Whatever you ask in my name, this I will do, that the Father may be glorified in the Son. If you ask me anything in my name, I will do it."

Jeremiah 33:3
Call to me and I will answer you, and will tell you great and hidden things that you have not known.

Ephesians 6:18
… praying at all times in the Spirit, with all prayer and supplication. To that end keep alert with all perseverance, making supplication for all the saints …

James 4:2b–3
You do not have, because you do not ask. You ask and do not receive, because you ask wrongly, to spend it on your passions.

James 5:16
Therefore, confess your sins to one another and pray for one another, that you may be healed. The prayer of a righteous person has great power as it is working.

1 Thessalonians 5:17
… pray without ceasing …

Matthew 6:6–8
"But when you pray, go into your room and shut the door and pray to your Father who is in secret. And your Father who sees in secret will reward you.

"And when you pray, do not heap up empty phrases as the Gentiles do, for they think that they will be heard for their many words. Do not be like them, for your Father knows what you need before you ask him."

John 16:24
"Until now you have asked nothing in my name. Ask, and you will receive, that your joy may be full."

Luke 11:9
"And I tell you, ask, and it will be given to you; seek, and you will find; knock, and it will be opened to you."

Matthew 21:22
"And whatever you ask in prayer, you will receive, if you have faith."

Putting Others First (Serving Others)

Mark 10:43–45
"But it shall not be so among you. But whoever would be great among you must be your servant, and whoever would be first among you must be slave of all. For even the Son of Man came not to be served but to serve, and to give his life as a ransom for many."

John 13:3–5
Jesus, knowing that the Father had given all things into his hands, and that he had come from God and was going back

to God, rose from supper. He laid aside his outer garments, and taking a towel, tied it around his waist. Then he poured water into a basin and began to wash the disciples' feet and to wipe them with the towel that was wrapped around him.

Luke 22:25–27
And he said to them, "The kings of the Gentiles exercise lordship over them, and those in authority over them are called benefactors. But not so with you. Rather, let the greatest among you become as the youngest, and the leader as one who serves. For who is the greater, one who reclines at table or one who serves? Is it not the one who reclines at table? But I am among you as the one who serves."

Philippians 2:7
… but [Jesus] made himself nothing, taking the form of a servant, being born in the likeness of men.

John 13:34–35
"A new commandment I give to you, that you love one another: just as I have loved you, you also are to love one another. By this all people will know that you are my disciples, if you have love for one another."

Romans 12:10
Love one another with brotherly affection. Outdo one another in showing honor.

Galatians 5:13
For you were called to freedom, brothers. Only do not use your freedom as an opportunity for the flesh, but through love serve one another.

Galatians 6:2
Bear one another's burdens, and so fulfill the law of Christ.

1 Peter 4:10
As each has received a gift, use it to serve one another, as good stewards of God's varied grace …

The Return of Christ

John 14:3
"And if I go and prepare a place for you, I will come again and will take you to myself, that where I am you may be also."

Luke 12:40
"You also must be ready, for the Son of Man is coming at an hour you do not expect."

Matthew 24:36
"But concerning that day and hour no one knows, not even the angels of heaven, nor the Son, but the Father only."

Acts 1:11
… and said, "Men of Galilee, why do you stand looking into heaven? This Jesus, who was taken up from you into heaven, will come in the same way as you saw him go into heaven."

1 Thessalonians 4:16–17
For the Lord himself will descend from heaven with a cry of command, with the voice of an archangel, and with the sound of the trumpet of God. And the dead in Christ will rise first. Then we who are alive, who are left, will be caught up together with them in the clouds to meet the Lord in the air, and so we will always be with the Lord.

1 Corinthians 15:51–52
Behold! I tell you a mystery. We shall not all sleep, but we shall all be changed, in a moment, in the twinkling of an eye, at the last trumpet. For the trumpet will sound, and the dead will be raised imperishable, and we shall be changed.

1 John 3:2
Beloved, we are God's children now, and what we will be has not yet appeared; but we know that when he appears we shall be like him, because we shall see him as he is.

1 Thessalonians 4:16
For the Lord himself will descend from heaven with a cry of command, with the voice of an archangel, and with the sound of the trumpet of God. And the dead in Christ will rise first.

Hebrews 9:28
… so Christ, having been offered once to bear the sins of many, will appear a second time, not to deal with sin but to save those who are eagerly waiting for him.

Satan

James 4:7
Submit yourselves therefore to God. Resist the devil, and he will flee from you.

Ephesians 4:27
… and give no opportunity to the devil.

1 Peter 5:8
Be sober-minded; be watchful. Your adversary the devil

prowls around like a roaring lion, seeking someone to devour.

Isaiah 14:12–14
"How you are fallen from heaven,
    O Day Star, son of Dawn!
How you are cut down to the ground,
    you who laid the nations low!
You said in your heart,
    'I will ascend to heaven;
    above the stars of God
    I will set my throne on high;
    I will sit on the mount of assembly
    in the far reaches of the north;
I will ascend above the heights of the clouds;
    I will make myself like the Most High.'"

John 8:44
"You are of your father the devil, and your will is to do your father's desires. He was a murderer from the beginning, and has nothing to do with the truth, because there is no truth in him. When he lies, he speaks out of his own character, for he is a liar and the father of lies."

1 John 3:8
Whoever makes a practice of sinning is of the devil, for the devil has been sinning from the beginning. The reason the Son of God appeared was to destroy the works of the devil.

Servanthood (see *Putting Others First*)

Sex

Psalm 119:73
Your hands have made and fashioned me;
   give me understanding that I may learn your
      commandments.

Hebrews 13:4
Let marriage be held in honor among all, and let the
marriage bed be undefiled, for God will judge the sexually
immoral and adulterous.

1 Corinthians 6:13
"Food is meant for the stomach and the stomach for
food"—and God will destroy both one and the other. The
body is not meant for sexual immorality, but for the Lord,
and the Lord for the body.

Romans 13:13
Let us walk properly as in the daytime, not in orgies and
drunkenness, not in sexual immorality and sensuality, not
in quarreling and jealousy.

1 Corinthians 6:18
Flee from sexual immorality. Every other sin a person
commits is outside the body, but the sexually immoral
person sins against his own body.

Genesis 2:24
Therefore a man shall leave his father and his mother and
hold fast to his wife, and they shall become one flesh.

1 Corinthians 7:9
But if they cannot exercise self-control, they should marry.
For it is better to marry than to be aflame with passion.

1 Corinthians 7:4–5
For the wife does not have authority over her own body, but the husband does. Likewise the husband does not have authority over his own body, but the wife does. Do not deprive one another, except perhaps by agreement for a limited time, that you may devote yourselves to prayer; but then come together again, so that Satan may not tempt you because of your lack of self-control.

Galatians 5:19
Now the works of the flesh are evident: sexual immorality, impurity, sensuality ...

Romans 1:26–27
For this reason God gave them up to dishonorable passions. For their women exchanged natural relations for those that are contrary to nature; and the men likewise gave up natural relations with women and were consumed with passion for one another, men committing shameless acts with men and receiving in themselves the due penalty for their error.

Leviticus 18:22
You shall not lie with a male as with a woman; it is an abomination.

1 John 2:3
And by this we know that we have come to know him, if we keep his commandments.

Sharing Your Faith

Matthew 28:18–20
And Jesus came and said to them, "All authority in heaven and on earth has been given to me. Go therefore and make disciples of all nations, baptizing them in the name of the Father and of the Son and of the Holy Spirit, teaching them to observe all that I have commanded you. And behold, I am with you always, to the end of the age."

Acts 1:8
"But you will receive power when the Holy Spirit has come upon you, and you will be my witnesses in Jerusalem and in all Judea and Samaria, and to the end of the earth."

Romans 10:14–15
But how are they to call on him in whom they have not believed? And how are they to believe in him of whom they have never heard? And how are they to hear without someone preaching? And how are they to preach unless they are sent? As it is written, "How beautiful are the feet of those who preach the good news!"

1 Peter 3:15
… but in your hearts regard Christ the Lord as holy, always being prepared to make a defense to anyone who asks you for a reason for the hope that is in you …

Matthew 5:16
"In the same way, let your light shine before others, so that they may see your good works and give glory to your Father who is in heaven."

Acts 20:24
But I do not account my life of any value nor as precious to

myself, if only I may finish my course and the ministry that I received from the Lord Jesus, to testify to the gospel of the grace of God.

Colossians 4:5
Conduct yourselves wisely toward outsiders, making the best use of the time.

Acts 22:15
"… for you will be a witness for him to everyone of what you have seen and heard."

Proverbs 11:30
The fruit of the righteous is a tree of life,
    and whoever captures souls is wise.

Sin

Ecclesiastes 7:20
Surely there is not a righteous man on earth who does good and never sins.

Romans 3:10–12
… as it is written:
"None is righteous, no, not one;
    no one understands;
    no one seeks for God.
All have turned aside; together they have become worthless;
    no one does good,
    not even one."

James 4:17
So whoever knows the right thing to do and fails to do it,

for him it is sin.

1 John 1:7–9
But if we walk in the light, as he is in the light, we have fellowship with one another, and the blood of Jesus his Son cleanses us from all sin. If we say we have no sin, we deceive ourselves, and the truth is not in us. If we confess our sins, he is faithful and just to forgive us our sins and to cleanse us from all unrighteousness.

Romans 6:23
For the wages of sin is death, but the free gift of God is eternal life in Christ Jesus our Lord.

Matthew 18:8
"And if your hand or your foot causes you to sin, cut it off and throw it away. It is better for you to enter life crippled or lame than with two hands or two feet to be thrown into the eternal fire."

Proverbs 28:13
Whoever conceals his transgressions will not prosper,
 but he who confesses and forsakes them will obtain
  mercy.

James 1:15
Then desire when it has conceived gives birth to sin, and sin when it is fully grown brings forth death.

1 John 3:4
Everyone who makes a practice of sinning also practices lawlessness; sin is lawlessness.

Speech

James 3:2
For we all stumble in many ways, and if anyone does not stumble in what he says, he is a perfect man, able also to bridle his whole body.

Ecclesiastes 10:20
Even in your thought, do not curse the king,
    nor in your bedroom curse the rich,
for a bird of the air will carry your voice,
    or some winged creature tell the matter.

Colossians 3:8
But now you must put them all away: anger, wrath, malice, slander, and obscene talk from your mouth.

Proverbs 16:27–28
A worthless man plots evil,
    and his speech is like a scorching fire.
A dishonest man spreads strife,
    and a whisperer separates close friends.

Proverbs 26:20
For lack of wood the fire goes out,
    and where there is no whisperer, quarreling ceases.

Proverbs 26:28
A lying tongue hates its victims,
    and a flattering mouth works ruin.

Proverbs 27:2
Let another praise you, and not your own mouth;
    a stranger, and not your own lips.

James 3:9–10
With it we bless our Lord and Father, and with it we curse people who are made in the likeness of God. From the same mouth come blessing and cursing. My brothers, these things ought not to be so.

Ephesians 4:29
Let no corrupting talk come out of your mouths, but only such as is good for building up, as fits the occasion, that it may give grace to those who hear.

Substance Abuse

John 8:34–36
Jesus answered them, "Truly, truly, I say to you, everyone who commits sin is a slave to sin. The slave does not remain in the house forever; the son remains forever. So if the Son sets you free, you will be free indeed."

Ephesians 6:12
For we do not wrestle against flesh and blood, but against the rulers, against the authorities, against the cosmic powers over this present darkness, against the spiritual forces of evil in the heavenly places.

Luke 4:18
"The Spirit of the Lord is upon me,
   because he has anointed me to proclaim good news to
      the poor.
   He has sent me to proclaim liberty to the captives and
      recovering of sight to the blind,
   to set at liberty those who are oppressed ..."

1 Corinthians 6:12
"All things are lawful for me," but not all things are helpful.
"All things are lawful for me," but I will not be enslaved by
anything.

John 8:31–32
So Jesus said to the Jews who had believed in him, "If you
abide in my word, you are truly my disciples, and you will
know the truth, and the truth will set you free."

2 Peter 2:19
They promise them freedom, but they themselves are
slaves of corruption. For whatever overcomes a person, to
that he is enslaved.

Romans 8:15
For you did not receive the spirit of slavery to fall back into
fear, but you have received the Spirit of adoption as sons, by
whom we cry, "Abba! Father!"

Romans 6:11–14
So you also must consider yourselves dead to sin and alive
to God in Christ Jesus.
    Let not sin therefore reign in your mortal bodies,
to make you obey their passions. Do not present your
members to sin as instruments for unrighteousness,
but present yourselves to God as those who have been
brought from death to life, and your members to God
as instruments for righteousness. For sin will have no
dominion over you, since you are not under law but under
grace.

1 Corinthians 9:27
But I discipline my body and keep it under control, lest
after preaching to others I myself should be disqualified.

2 Corinthians 3:17
Now the Lord is the Spirit, and where the Spirit of the Lord is, there is freedom.

Galatians 5:1
For freedom Christ has set us free; stand firm therefore, and do not submit again to a yoke of slavery.

Galatians 5:13
For you were called to freedom, brothers. Only do not use your freedom as an opportunity for the flesh, but through love serve one another.

Temptation

1 Corinthians 10:12–13
Therefore let anyone who thinks that he stands take heed lest he fall. No temptation has overtaken you that is not common to man. God is faithful, and he will not let you be tempted beyond your ability, but with the temptation he will also provide the way of escape, that you may be able to endure it.

Hebrews 4:15
For we do not have a high priest who is unable to sympathize with our weaknesses, but one who in every respect has been tempted as we are, yet without sin.

James 1:13–15
Let no one say when he is tempted, "I am being tempted by God," for God cannot be tempted with evil, and he himself tempts no one. But each person is tempted when he is lured and enticed by his own desire. Then desire when it

has conceived gives birth to sin, and sin when it is fully grown brings forth death.

Ephesians 6:16
In all circumstances take up the shield of faith, with which you can extinguish all the flaming darts of the evil one …

Hebrews 2:18
For because he himself has suffered when tempted, he is able to help those who are being tempted.

James 4:7
Submit yourselves therefore to God. Resist the devil, and he will flee from you.

1 Corinthians 15:33–34
Do not be deceived: "Bad company ruins good morals." Wake up from your drunken stupor, as is right, and do not go on sinning. For some have no knowledge of God. I say this to your shame.

2 Peter 2:9
… then the Lord knows how to rescue the godly from trials, and to keep the unrighteous under punishment until the day of judgment …

2 Timothy 2:22
So flee youthful passions and pursue righteousness, faith, love, and peace, along with those who call on the Lord from a pure heart.

Psalm 101:3–4
I will not set before my eyes
    anything that is worthless.
I hate the work of those who fall away;
    it shall not cling to me.

A perverse heart shall be far from me;
  I will know nothing of evil.

1 Peter 5:8–10
Be sober-minded; be watchful. Your adversary the devil
prowls around like a roaring lion, seeking someone to
devour. Resist him, firm in your faith, knowing that the
same kinds of suffering are being experienced by your
brotherhood throughout the world. And after you have
suffered a little while, the God of all grace, who has called
you to his eternal glory in Christ, will himself restore,
confirm, strengthen, and establish you.

Romans 6:14
For sin will have no dominion over you, since you are not
under law but under grace.

Tough Times

James 1:2–4
Count it all joy, my brothers, when you meet trials of
various kinds, for you know that the testing of your faith
produces steadfastness. And let steadfastness have its full
effect, that you may be perfect and complete, lacking in
nothing.

2 Timothy 2:3
Share in suffering as a good soldier of Christ Jesus.

Psalm 50:15
"… and call upon me in the day of trouble;
  I will deliver you, and you shall glorify me."

Hebrews 12:1–2
Therefore, since we are surrounded by so great a cloud of witnesses, let us also lay aside every weight, and sin which clings so closely, and let us run with endurance the race that is set before us, looking to Jesus, the founder and perfecter of our faith, who for the joy that was set before him endured the cross, despising the shame, and is seated at the right hand of the throne of God.

Psalm 9:9–10
The Lord is a stronghold for the oppressed,
    a stronghold in times of trouble.
And those who know your name put their trust in you,
    for you, O Lord, have not forsaken those who seek you.

Psalm 34:18
The Lord is near to the brokenhearted
    and saves the crushed in spirit.

Psalm 30:5
For his anger is but for a moment,
    and his favor is for a lifetime.
Weeping may tarry for the night,
    but joy comes with the morning.

Psalm 119:28
My soul melts away for sorrow;
    strengthen me according to your word!

Lamentations 3:31–33
For the Lord will not cast off forever,
but, though he cause grief, he will have compassion
        according to the abundance of his steadfast love;
for he does not willingly afflict
    or grieve the children of men.

1 Peter 4:12–13
Beloved, do not be surprised at the fiery trial when it comes
upon you to test you, as though something strange were
happening to you. But rejoice insofar as you share Christ's
sufferings, that you may also rejoice and be glad when his
glory is revealed.

1 Peter 5:10
And after you have suffered a little while, the God of all
grace, who has called you to his eternal glory in Christ, will
himself restore, confirm, strengthen, and establish you.

Jeremiah 29:11
For I know the plans I have for you, declares the LORD,
plans for wholeness and not for evil, to give you a future
and a hope.

Witnessing (see *Sharing Your Faith*)

WORK

Genesis 2:15
The LORD God took the man and put him in the garden of
Eden to work it and keep it.

Proverbs 28:19
Whoever works his land will have plenty of bread,
    but he who follows worthless pursuits will have plenty of
        poverty.

Ephesians 4:28
Let the thief no longer steal, but rather let him labor, doing honest work with his own hands, so that he may have something to share with anyone in need.

Colossians 3:23–24
Whatever you do, work heartily, as for the Lord and not for men knowing that from the Lord you will receive the inheritance as your reward. You are serving the Lord Christ.

Proverbs 22:29
Do you see a man skillful in his work?
    He will stand before kings;
    he will not stand before obscure men.

Proverbs 6:6
Go to the ant, O sluggard;
    consider her ways, and be wise.

Proverbs 6:10–11
A little sleep, a little slumber,
    a little folding of the hands to rest,
and poverty will come upon you like a robber,
    and want like an armed man.

Proverbs 20:13
Love not sleep, lest you come to poverty;
    open your eyes, and you will have plenty of bread.

Proverbs 13:4
The soul of the sluggard craves and gets nothing,
    while the soul of the diligent is richly supplied.

Proverbs 10:4–5
A slack hand causes poverty,
    but the hand of the diligent makes rich.

He who gathers in summer is a prudent son,
  but he who sleeps in harvest is a son who brings shame.

Galatians 6:4–5
But let each one test his own work, and then his reason to boast will be in himself alone and not in his neighbor. For each will have to bear his own load.

Proverbs 14:23
In all toil there is profit,
  but mere talk tends only to poverty.

APPENDIX I:

Where Do I Find...?

The Creation	Genesis 1–2
The Fall of Man	Genesis 3
The Flood and Noah's Ark	Genesis 6–9
The Ten Commandments	Exodus 20:1–17
The Shepherd's Psalm	Psalm 23
The Christmas Story	Luke 2:1–20 and Matthew 1:18–2:12
The Sermon on the Mount	Matthew 5–7
The Golden Rule	Matthew 7:12
The Lord's Prayer	Luke 11:1–4
The Greatest Commandment	Matthew 22:36–40
Christ's Commandment	John 13:34
The Crucifixion and Resurrection	Mark 15–16
The Great Commission	Matthew 28:19–20
Christ's Ascension	Acts 1:1–9
The Conversion of Paul	Acts 9
Spiritual Gifts	Romans 12:3–8; 1 Corinthians 12:7–10, 28–30; Ephesians 4:4–8, 11–13
The Fruit of the Spirit	Galatians 5:22–26
The Love Chapter	1 Corinthians 13

APPENDIX 2:

Important Verses You Should Know

2 Timothy 3:16–17 (why the Bible's important)

Colossians 1:15–20 (who is Christ?)

Genesis 1:27 (the creation of mankind)

Ecclesiastes 7:20 (the truth about mankind)

Romans 3:23 (the plight of mankind)

John 3:16–17 (the Bible in miniature)

Romans 1:20 (what about those who haven't heard about Jesus?)

Romans 6:23 (the result of sin)

1 Thessalonians 5:17 (a good rule of thumb)

Ephesians 2:8–10 (how and why we were saved)

John 1:12–13 (how to become a Christian)

1 John 1:9 (how to be forgiven)

Psalm 103:12 (how completely God forgives)

1 John 5:11–12 (how to know if you are a Christian)

2 Corinthians 5:17 (the new life)

John 17:3 (the definition of eternal life)

Hebrews 11:1 (the definition of faith)

Acts 16:30–31 ("What must I do to be saved?")

Colossians 4:5 (how to share your faith)

Matthew 24:36 (when is Jesus coming back?)

Acts 4:12 (Jesus is the only way)

Matthew 6:33 (get your priorities straight!)

Colossians 2:8 (stay strong intellectually)

Hosea 6:6 (what God likes, part I)

Micah 6:8 (what God likes, part II)

Deuteronomy 5:32–33 (the benefit of obeying God)

Hebrews 12:5–6 (when God disciplines you)

John 13:34–35 (the ultimate witness)

Psalm 27:1–2 (we have no one to fear)

James 1:2–4 (trials and tribulations)

Romans 8:28 (when life gives you lemons)

Ephesians 1:7–8 (the richness of God's grace)

Philippians 1:6 (God's working on me!)

Joshua 1:8–9 (be courageous)

Isaiah 53:6 (Jesus in the Old Testament)

Romans 12:1–2 (God's recipe for successful living)

Philippians 4:13 (Christ's strength in us)

1 Corinthians 10:13 (for when you are tempted)

James 4:2 (encouragement to pray)

Galatians 2:20 (our new life)

Jeremiah 33:3 (call upon God)

Hebrews 10:24–25 (stay in fellowship)

Matthew 28:19–20 (Christ's Great Commission)

Psalm 46:10 (a good reminder when you're stressed)

James 5:16 (the power of prayer)

John 14:6 (who Jesus says He is)

APPENDIX 3:
You Heard it Here First

Many words and phrases in the English language first appeared in the Bible. Still others became common because of their use in Scripture. Here are several:

in the beginning (Genesis 1:1)

let there be light (Genesis 1:3)

my brother's keeper (Genesis 4:9)

to put words in his mouth (Exodus 4:15)

eye for an eye, tooth for a tooth (Exodus 21:24)

scapegoat (Leviticus 16:8)

to fall flat on his face (Numbers 22:31)

the skin of my teeth (Job 19:20)

the land of the living (Job 28:13)

to stand in awe (Psalm 4:4)

out of the mouth of babes (Psalm 8:2)

the apple of your eye (Psalm 17:8)

to pour out one's heart (Psalm 62:8)

to go from strength to strength (Psalm 84:7)

pride goes before a fall (Proverbs 16:18)

under the sun (Ecclesiastes 1:14)

a fly in the ointment (Ecclesiastes 10:1)

swords into plowshares (Isaiah 2:4)

a drop in the bucket (Isaiah 40:15)

like a lamb to the slaughter (Isaiah 53:7)

rise and shine (Isaiah 60:1)

from time to time (Ezekiel 4:10)

sour grapes (Exekiel 18:2)

the writing on the wall (Daniel 5:5)

into the lions' den (Daniel 6:17–24)

the salt of the earth (Matthew 5:13)

go the extra mile (Matthew 5:41)

seek and you will find (Matthew 7:7)

wolf in sheep's clothing (Matthew 7:15)

live by the sword, die by the sword (Matthew 26:51–52)

and it came to pass (Mark 1:9)

to give up the ghost (Mark 15:37)

turn the other cheek (Luke 6:29)

eat, drink, and be merry (Luke 12:19)

prodigal son (Luke 15:11–32)

the truth shall set you free (John 8:32)

the scales fell from his eyes (Acts 9:18)

the powers that be (Romans 13:1)

a thorn in the flesh (2 Corinthians 12:7)

[Sources include *In the Beginning*, by Alister McGrath. The wording in your own Bible may differ from the colloquialisms listed here.]

A Final Word

We hope that this book has encouraged you to explore the Bible and that God's Word will ultimately point you to Christ, the Author of life and Perfecter of our faith. As He Himself said,

> *You search the Scriptures because you think that in them you have eternal life; and it is they that bear witness about me ... come to me that you may have life.* (John 5:39–40)

May you experience life to the fullest through Christ!

COLOPHON
Created using Adobe InDesign CS2 and Accordance software
Composed primarily in Scala and Scala Sans, typefaces designed by Martin Majoor in 1994
Main text size is 11.5 points; topic titles range from 20 to 30 points
Cover photos @ Stephen Boks. Used with permission

You might also enjoy these other books from Whitecaps Media

Take a daily passage through Mark with John Wayland

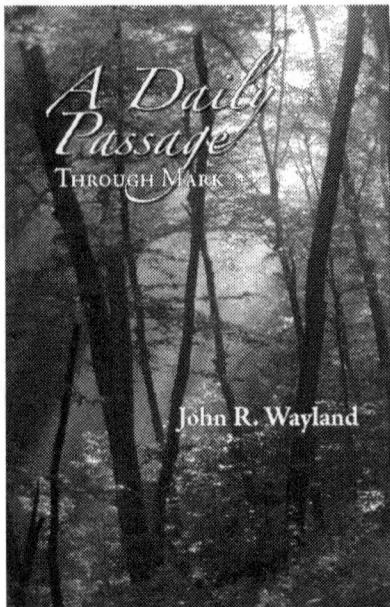

In his first book, *A Daily Passage Through Mark*, John Wayland takes the reader through the entire Gospel of Mark in a series of 109 daily readings. Written in Wayland's unique heartfelt manner, this book combines solid theology with practical, everyday application.

Wayland is a graduate of Southwestern University in Georgetown, Texas, as well as Dallas Theological Seminary. He serves as senior pastor of Northwest Bible Church in Spring, Texas (outside of Houston). For sixteen years John was on the staff of Young Life.

Available at
www.whitecapsmedia.com

**Everybody's faith could use a
jumpstart from time to time**

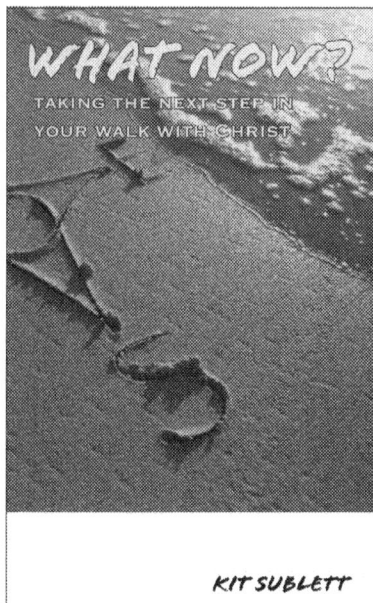

Whether you are in high school or in middle age, or somewhere in between, you might find yourself asking, "What now? I already have a relationship with Jesus, but I want it to be deeper." If that describes you, then you're who this book was written for.

After twenty years of working with young Christians while on the staff of Young Life, Kit Sublett has written this excellent book to help Christians of all ages and stages go deeper in their faith and take their next step with Christ.

Whitecaps Media
P. O. Box 60385
Houston, TX 77205-0385